Non-Religious
for Naming Ce

Compiled by Hugh Morrison

Montpelier Publishing
London
MMXV

ISBN-13: 978-1511993364
ISBN-10: 1511993367
Published by Montpelier Publishing, London.
Printed by Amazon Createspace.
Cover image by Vera Kratochvil.

To a Child

If by any device or knowledge,
The rosebud its beauty could know,
It would stay a rosebud for ever,
Nor into its fullness grow.

And if thou could'st know thy own sweetness,
O little one, perfect and sweet!
Thou wouldst be a child for ever,
Completer whilst incomplete.

Francis Turner Palgrave

My Little Dear

My little dear, so fast asleep,
Whose arms about me cling,
What kisses shall she have to keep,
While she is slumbering?

Upon her golden baby-hair,
The golden dreams I'll kiss
Which Life spread through my morning fair,
And I have saved, for this.

Upon her baby eyes I'll press
The kiss Love gave to me,
When his great joy and loveliness
Made all things fair to see.

And on her lips, with smiles astir,
Ah me, what prayer of old
May now be kissed to comfort her,
Should Love or Life grow cold.

Dollie Radford

Apache Blessing

May the sun bring you new energy by day,
May the moon softly restore you by night,
May the rain wash away your worries
And the breeze blow new strength into your being,
And all of the days of your life may you walk
Gently through the world and know its beauty.

Infant Joy

'I have no name;
I am but two days old.'
What shall I call thee?

'I happy am,
Joy is my name.'
Sweet joy befall thee!
Pretty joy!

Sweet joy, but two days old.
Sweet Joy I call thee:
Thou dost smile,
I sing the while;
Sweet joy befall thee!

William Blake

Be True to Those Who Trust Thee

Be true to those who trust thee,
Be pure for those who care.
Be strong, for there is much to suffer,
Be brave, for there is much to dare.
Be a friend to all – the foe, the friendless.
Be giving and forget the gift.
Be humble, for thou knowest thy weakness.
And then, look up and laugh and love and live.

Anon

Babyhood

A baby shines as bright
If winter or if May be
On eyes that keep in sight
A baby.

Though dark the skies or grey be,
It fills our eyes with light,
If midnight or midday be.
Love hails it, day and night,
The sweetest thing that may be,
Yet cannot praise aright
A baby.

Algernon Charles Swinburne

Spirit of the Child

Give us the child who lives within – the child who trusts, the child who imagines, the child who sings, the child who receives without reservation, the child who gives without judgement.
Give us a child's eyes, that we may receive the beauty and freshness of this day like a sunrise.
Give us a child's ears, that we may hear the music of mythical times.
Give us a child's heart, that we may be filled with wonder and delight.
Give us a child's faith, that we may be cured of our cynicism.
Give us the spirit of the child, who is not afraid to need, who is not afraid to love.

Anon

Cradle Songs

Baby, baby bright,
Sleep can steal from sight
Little of your light:

Soft as fire in dew,
Still the life in you
Lights your slumber through.

Four white eyelids keep
Fast the seal of sleep
Deep as love is deep:

Yet, though closed it lies,
Love behind them spies
Heaven in two blue eyes.

Baby, baby dear,
Earth and heaven are near
Now, for heaven is here.

Heaven is every place
Where your flower-sweet face
Fills our eyes with grace.

Till your own eyes deign
Earth a glance again,
Earth and heaven are twain.

Now your sleep is done,
Shine, and show the sun
Earth and heaven are one.

Algernon Charles Swinburne

Footprints

'Walk a little slower Daddy' said a child so small
'I'm following in your footsteps and I don't want to fall.
Sometimes your steps are very fast,
Sometimes they're hard to see;
So walk a little slower Daddy,
For you are leading me.
Someday when I'm all grown up,
You're what I want to be;
Then I will have a little child
Who'll want to follow me.
And I would want to lead just right,
And know that I was true;
So walk a little slower Daddy,
For I must follow you.

Anon

A Poem For Parents

There are little eyes upon you,
And they are watching night and day;
There are little ears that quickly
Take in every word you say.

There are little hands all eager
To do everything you do;
And a little boy who's dreaming
Of the day he'll be like you.

You're the little fellow's idol;
You're the wisest of the wise;
In his little mind, about you
No suspicions ever rise.

He believes in you devotedly,
Holds that all you say and do,
He will say and do in your way
When he's grown up like you.

There's a wide-eyed little fellow
Who believes you're always right;
And his ears are always open,
And he watches day and night.

You are setting an example
Every day in all you do;
For the little boy who's waiting
To grow up to be just like you.

Anon

Babies are Angels

Babies are angels that fly to the earth,
Their wings disappear at the time of their birth.
One look in their eyes and we're never the same,
They're part of us now and that part has a name.
That part is your heart and a bond that won't sever,
Our babies are angels, we love them forever.

Anon

From **Twins**

April, on whose wings
Ride all gracious tidings,
Like the star that brings
All tidings good to man,
Ere his light, that yet
Makes the month shine, set,
And fair May forget
Whence her birth began,

Brings, as heart would choose,
Sound of golden news,
Bright as kindling dews
When the dawn begins ;
Tidings clear as mirth,
Sweet as air and earth
Now that hail the birth,
Twice thus blest, of twins.

In the lovely land
Where with hand in hand
Lovers wedded stand
Other joys before
Made your mixed life sweet:
Now, as Time sees meet,
Three glad blossoms greet
Two glad blossoms more.

Algernon Charles Swinburne

An Irish Blessing

May green be the grass you walk on,
May blue be the skies above you,
May pure be the joys that surround you,
May true be the hearts that love you.

Étude Réaliste

I

A baby's feet, like sea-shells pink,
Might tempt, should Heaven see meet,
An angel's lips to kiss, we think,
 A baby's feet.
Like rose-hued sea-flowers toward the heat
They stretch and spread and wink
Their ten soft buds that part and meet.
No flower-bells that expand and shrink
Gleam half so heavenly sweet
As shine on life's untrodden brink
A baby's feet.

II

A baby's hands, like rosebuds furl'd,
Whence yet no leaf expands,
Ope if you touch, though close upcurl'd,
A baby's hands.
Then, even as warriors grip their brands
When battle's bolt is hurl'd,
They close, clench'd hard like tightening bands.
No rosebuds yet by dawn impearl'd
Match, even in loveliest lands,
The sweetest flowers in all the world—
A baby's hands.

III

A baby's eyes, ere speech begin,
Ere lips learn words or sighs,
Bless all things bright enough to win
A baby's eyes.
Love, while the sweet thing laughs and lies,
And sleep flows out and in,
Lies perfect in them Paradise.

Their glance might cast out pain and sin,
Their speech make dumb the wise,
By mute glad godhead felt within
A baby's eyes.

Algernon Charles Swinburne

An Old Irish Blessing

May love and laughter light your days,
And warm your heart and home.
May good and faithful friends be yours,
Wherever you may roam.
May peace and plenty bless your world
With joy that long endures.
May all life's passing seasons
Bring the best to you and yours!

Life Is

Life is an opportunity; benefit from it.
Life is a beauty; admire it.
Life is a dream; realise it.
Life is a challenge; meet it.
Life is a duty; complete it.
Life is a game; play it.
Life is a promise; fulfill it.
Life is sorrow; overcome it.
Life is a song; sing it.
Life is a struggle; accept it.
Life is a tragedy; confront it.
Life is an adventure; dare it.
Life is luck; make it.
Life is life; fight for it!

Mother Teresa of Calcutta

The Child-Angel

They clamour and fight, they doubt and despair, they know no end to their wrangling.

Let your life come amongst them like a flame of light, my child, unflickering and pure, and delight them into silence.

They are cruel in their greed and their envy, their words are like hidden knives thirsting for blood.

Go and stand amidst their scowling hearts, my child, and let your gentle eyes fall upon them like the forgiving peace of the evening over the strife of the day.

Let them see your face, my child, and thus know the meaning of all things; let them love you and thus love each other.

Come and take your seat in the bosom of the limitless, my child. At sunrise open and raise your heart like a blossoming flower, and at sunset bend your head and in silence complete the worship of the day.

Rabindranath Tagore

From **To a Child**

O child! O new-born denizen
Of life's great city! on thy head
The glory of the morn is shed,
Like a celestial benison!
Here at the portal thou dost stand,
And with thy little hand
Thou openest the mysterious gate
Into the future's undiscovered land.
I see its valves expand,
As at the touch of Fate!
Into those realms of love and hate,
Into that darkness blank and drear.
By some prophetic feeling taught,
I launch the bold, adventurous thought,
Freighted with hope and fear;
As upon subterranean streams.
In caverns unexplored and dark,
Men sometimes launch a fragile bark.
Laden with flickering fire.
And watch its swift-receding beams,
Until at length they disappear,
And in the distant dark expire.

By what astrology of fear or hope
Dare I to cast thy horoscope!
Like the new moon thy life appears;
A little strip of silver light,
And widening outward into night
The shadowy disk of future years;
And yet upon its outer rim,
A luminous circle, faint and dim,
And scarcely visible to us here,
Rounds and completes the perfect sphere.

Henry Wadsworth Longfellow

A Mother's Song

Peace rest on thine eyelids,
As sweetly they close,
And thoughts of to-morrow
Ne'er break thy repose.
What dreams in thy slumber
Dear baby, are thine?
Thy sweet lips are smiling
When pressed thus to mine.
All lovely and guileless
Thou sleepest in joy.
And Heaven watches over my beautiful boy
Oh, would thus that ever
My darling might smile,
And still be a baby
My griefs to beguile;
But hope whispers sweetly,
'Ne'er broken shall be
The tie that unites my sweet baby to me.'

Alexander Smart

My Treasure

Fairest among children fair,
Is the baby that I bear
On my bosom, like a dove
Nestling in its home of love.
Oh, to me he's always fair;
Winsome babe, my love and care.
But, when sleep with magic spell
Lures my babe where angels dwell,
Then, in rapture and amaze,
On his lovely face I gaze,
Lingering long beside the bed,
Stroking oft the silken head —
Pressing many a long fond kiss
On his lips, so thrilled with bliss.
That for very joy I weep.
Over baby, fast asleep.
Oh, how sweet my cup of life!
Happy mother, happy wife!
Naught can drain my cup of joy.
While my arms enfold my boy.

Anon

Baby Skies

Would you know the baby skies?
Baby's skies are mother's eyes.
Mother's eyes and smile together
Make the baby's pleasant weather.
Mother, keep your eyes from tears
Keep your heart from foolish fears
Keep your lips from dull complaining
Lest the baby think 'tis raining.

Mary C. Bartlett.

Baby Mine

Baby mine, with the grave, grave face,
Where did you get that royal calm,
Too staid for joy, too still for grace?
I bend as I kiss your pink, soft palm;
Are you the first of a nobler race,
Baby mine?

You come from the region of long ago
And gazing awhile where the seraphs dwell
Has given your face a glory and a glow, —
Of that brighter land have you aught to tell?
I seem to have known it — I more would know,
Baby mine.

Your calm blue eyes have a far-off reach:
Look at me now with those wondrous eyes.
Why are we doom'd to the gift of speech
While you are silent and sweet and wise?
You have much to learn — you have more to teach,
Baby mine.

Frederick Locker

What is Home Without a Baby?

What is home without a baby,
With each gentle, winning way;
Sweet uplifted smiles inviting
Fond caresses all the day?
Darling baby,
Precious baby,
Give her kisses all the day.
Life is dull and duty pressing,
Care brings pain and weariness;
But the baby's soft embracing
Changes all our toil to bliss.
Darling baby,
Precious baby,
Like a ray of sunshine is.
How we watch each fond endeavour
After language, in her face;
Oh, what wealth of love we give her,
As her tiny steps we trace.
Darling baby,
Precious baby,
Adds to home a sweeter grace.

Anon

Children

Children are what mothers are.
No fondest father's fondest care
Can fashion so the infant heart
As those creative beams that dart,
With all their hopes and fears, upon
The cradle of a sleeping son.
His startled eyes with wonder see
A father near him on his knee,
Who wishes all the while to trace
The mother in his future face;
But 'tis to her alone uprise
His wakening arms; to her those eyes
Open with joy and not surprise.

Walter Savage Landor

Just as a mother would protect with her life her own son, her only son, so one should cultivate an unbounded mind towards all beings, and loving-kindness towards all the world.

One should cultivate an unbounded mind, above and below and across, without obstruction, without enmity, without rivalry.

Standing, or going, or seated, or lying down, as long as one is free from drowsiness, one should practice this mindfulness.

This, they say, is the holy state here.

Sutta Nipata (Buddhist scripture)

A Baby Rhyme

So new the skies, so new the bliss
Of baby fingers tender —
A weight so warm upon the arm,
A sleeping, breathing splendour;
O baby-bird! Sleep in thy nest,
Dear, warm, wee bird, sleep in thy nest.

Two hands clasped fast, two lids down cast.
Eyes — (brown or blue, which, mother?)
A heart as white as flowers at night,
Moon-kissed, that kissed each other;
Like birds at rest, so thou in nest
Sleep, baby-bird, sleep in thy nest.

So white the earth grew at thy birth
(Thy tiny feet were whiter) —
So light the fall of snow o'er all
(Thy warm home-nest was lighter);
O baby! Rest, in folded nest,
And sleep, sweet bird, within such nest.

But, baby dear, it is so queer,
Sometimes this world is clouded
And grey and grey, beneath the day,
It looks like friar shrouded.
But, little guest, sleep in thy nest,
Nor know the rest — sleep in thy nest.

And over thee, all warm I see
Two tear-bright eyes bend fondly;
And folded fast, upon thee cast,
Are kisses falling softly.
Then, bird at rest, within thy nest,
Sleep well, sleep well — sleep in the nest.

Oh, tiny thing without a wing!
Oh, bird with song yet hidden
The guest with glee would welcome thee
To life's feast later bidden;
And while the west calls day to rest,
We say, dear bird, sleep in thy nest.

Anon

Above all Price

How dear does mother hold
Her bonny little one?
Just as dear as the jostling clovers
Hold the merry sun.

How hard would mother try
To please her pretty lass?
Just as hard as the pattering showers
Try to please the grass.

How fair does mother think
The darling at her breast?
Just as fair as the glad white sea-bird
Thinks the wave's white crest.

How long will mother's love
For her treasure last?
Just as long as her heart keeps beating,
Till her life be past.

How much will mother's love
Change, as years are told?
Just as much as the mountain changes,
Or the ocean old.

Edgar Fawcett

All Mother

If I had an eagle's wings,
How grand to sail the sky!
But I should drop to the earth
If I heard my baby cry.

My baby — my darling,
The wings may go, for me!
If I were a splendid queen,
With a crown to keep in place,

Would it do for a little wet mouth
To rub all over my face?
My baby — my darling,
The crown may go, for me.

Anon

The Greatest Achievement

The greatest achievement is selflessness.
The greatest worth is self-mastery.
The greatest quality is seeking to serve others.
The greatest precept is continual awareness.
The greatest medicine is the emptiness of everything.
The greatest action is not conforming with the world's ways.
The greatest magic is transmuting the passions.
The greatest generosity is non-attachment.
The greatest goodness is a peaceful mind.
The greatest patience is humility.
The greatest effort is not concerned with results.
The greatest meditation is a mind that lets go.
The greatest wisdom is seeing through appearances.

Atisha

Baby

Dimpled and flushed and dewy pink he lies,
Crumpled and tossed and lapt in snowy bands;
Aimlessly reaching with his tiny hands,
Lifting in wondering gaze his great blue eyes.
Sweet pouting lips, parted by breathing sighs;
Soft cheeks, warm-tinted as from tropic lands;
Framed with brown hair in shining silken strands,—
All fair, all pure, a sunbeam from the skies!
O perfect innocence! O soul enshrined
In blissful ignorance of good or ill,
By never gale of idle passion crossed!
Although thou art no alien from thy kind,
Though pain and death may take thee captive, still
Through sin, at least, thine Eden is not lost.

Elaine Goodale Eastman

The New Arrival

There came to port last Sunday night,
The queerest little craft,
Without an inch of rigging on —
I looked, and looked, and laughed.

It was so singular that she
Should cross the unknown water,
And moor herself right in my room —
My daughter, oh, my daughter!

Yet by these presents witness all,
She's welcome fifty times,
And comes consigned to Hope and Love,
And common metre rhymes.

She has no manifest but this,
No flag floats o'er the water,
She's too new for the British Lloyds —
My daughter, oh, my daughter!

Ring out, wild bells — and tame ones too—
Ring out the lover's moon,
Ring out the little worsted socks,
Ring in the bib and spoon;

Ring out the muse, ring in the nurse,
Ring in the milk and water;
Away with paper, pens, and ink —
My daughter, oh, my daughter !

Anon

From **The Prophet**

And a woman who held a babe against her bosom said,
'Speak to us of Children.'
And he said:
'Your children are not your children.
They are the sons and daughters of Life's longing for itself.
They come through you but not from you,
And though they are with you, yet they belong not to you.
You may give them your love but not your thoughts.
For they have their own thoughts.
You may house their bodies but not their souls,
For their souls dwell in the house of tomorrow,
which you cannot visit, not even in your dreams.
You may strive to be like them, but seek not to make them like you.
For life goes not backward nor tarries with yesterday.
You are the bows from which your children as living arrows are sent
forth.
The archer sees the mark upon the path of the infinite,
and He bends you with His might that His arrows may go swift and
far.
Let your bending in the archer's hand be for gladness;
For even as he loves the arrow that flies,
so He loves also the bow that is stable.'

Kahlil Gibran

Baby's Way

If Baby only wanted to, he could fly up to heaven this moment.
It is not for nothing that he does not leave us.
He loves to rest his head on mother's bosom, and cannot ever bare to lose sight of her.
Baby knows all manner of wise words, though few on earth can understand their meaning.
It is not for nothing that he never wants to speak.
The one thing he wants is to learn mother's words from mother's lips.
That is why he looks so innocent.
Baby had a heap of gold and pearls, yet he came like a beggar on to this earth.
It is not for nothing he came in such a disguise.
This dear little naked mendicant pretends to be utterly helpless, so that he may beg for mother's wealth of love.
Baby was so free from every tie in the land of the tiny crescent moon.
It was not for nothing he gave up his freedom.
He knows that there is room for endless joy in mother's little corner of a heart, and it is sweeter far than liberty to be caught and pressed in her dear arms.
Baby never knew how to cry.
He dwelt in the land of perfect bliss.
It is not for nothing he has chosen to shed tears.
Though with the smile of his dear face he draws mother's yearning heart to him, yet his little cries over tiny troubles weave the double bond of pity and love.

Rabindranath Tagore

I am Love

Some say I can fly on the wind, yet I haven't any wings.
Some have found me floating on the open sea, yet I cannot swim.
Some have felt my warmth on cold nights, yet I have no flame.
And though you cannot see me,
I lay between two lovers at the hearth of fireplaces.
I am the twinkle in your child's eyes.
I am hidden in the lines of your mother's face.
I am your father's shield as he guards your home.
And yet… Some say I am stronger than steel, yet I am as fragile as a tear.
Some have never searched for me, yet I am around them always.
Some say I die with loss, yet I am endless.
And though you cannot hear me, I dance on the laughter of children.
I am woven into the whispers of passion.
I am in the blessings of Grandmothers.
I embrace the cries of newborn babies.
And yet…some say I am a flower, yet I am also the seed.
Some have little faith in me, yet I will always believe in them.
Some say I cannot cure the ill, yet I nourish the soul.
And though you cannot touch me, I am the gentle hand of the kind.
I am the fingertips that caress your cheek at night.
I am the hug of a child.
I am love.

Anon

A Baby Running Barefoot

When the bare feet of the baby beat across the grass
The little white feet nod like white flowers in the wind,
They poise and run like ripples lapping across the water;
And the sight of their white play among the grass
Is like a little robin's song, winsome,
Or as two white butterflies settle in the cup of one flower
For a moment, then away with a flutter of wings.
I long for the baby to wander hither to me
Like a wind-shadow wandering over the water,
So that she can stand on my knee
With her little bare feet in my hands,
Cool like syringa buds,
Firm and silken like pink young peony flowers.

D.H. Lawrence

Omaha Native American Children's Blessing

Sun, Moon, Stars, all you that move in the heavens, hear us!
Into your midst has come a new life.
Make his path smooth, that he may reach the brow of the first hill!
Winds, Clouds, Rain, Mist, all you that move in the air, hear us!
Into your midst has come a new life.
Make his path smooth, that he may reach the brow of the second
hill!
Hills, Valleys, Rivers, Lakes, Trees, Grasses, all you of the earth, hear
us!
Into your midst has come a new life.
Make his path smooth, that he may reach the brow of the third hill!
Birds, great and small, that fly in the air,
Animals, great and small, that dwell in the forest,
Insects that creep among the grasses and burrow in the ground,
hear us!
Into your midst has come a new life.
Make his path smooth, that he may reach the brow of the fourth
hill!
All you of the heavens, all you of the air, all you of the earth, hear
us!
Into your midst has come a new life.
Make his path smooth, then shall he travel beyond the four hills!

A Jewish Blessing

In every birth, blessed is the wonder.
In every creation, blessed is the new beginning.
In every child, blessed is life.
In every hope, blessed is the potential.
In every transition, blessed is the beginning.
In every existence, blessed are the possibilities.
In every love, blessed are the tears.
In every life, blessed is the love.
There are three names by which a person is called:
One which her father and mother call her,
And one which people call her,
And one which she earns for herself.
The best one of these is the one that she earns for herself.

From **A Child's Future**

What will it please you, my darling, hereafter to be?
Fame upon land will you look for, or glory by sea?
Gallant your life will be always, and all of it free.
Free as the wind when the heart of the twilight is stirred
Eastward, and sounds from the springs of the sunrise are heard:
Free and we know not another as infinite word.
Darkness or twilight or sunlight may compass us round,
Hate may arise up against us, or hope may confound;
Love may forsake us; yet may not the spirit be bound.
Free in oppression of grief as in ardour of joy
Still may the soul be, and each to her strength as a toy:
Free in the glance of the man as the smile of the boy.
Freedom alone is the salt and the spirit that gives
Life, and without her is nothing that verily lives:
Death cannot slay her: she laughs upon death and forgives.

Algernon Charles Swinburne

First Footsteps

A little way, more soft and sweet
Than fields aflower with May,
A babe's feet, venturing, scarce complete
A little way.
Eyes full of dawning day
Look up for mother's eyes to meet,
Too blithe for song to say.
Glad as the golden spring to greet
Its first live leaflet's play,
Love, laughing, leads the little feet
A little way.
Love, laughing, leads the little feet a little way

Algernon Charles Swinburne

A Blessing of St Patrick

May you be blessed with
The strength of heaven,
The light of the sun
And the radiance of the moon,
The splendour of fire,
The speed of lightning,
The swiftness of wind,
The depth of the sea,
The stability of earth,
And the firmness of rock.

The Salutation of the Dawn

Look to this day,
For it is life, the very life of life.
In its brief course lie all the varieties and realities of your existence:
The bliss of growth,
The glory of action,
The splendour of beauty:
For yesterday is but a dream
And tomorrow is only a vision,
But today well lived makes
Every yesterday a dream of happiness.
And every tomorrow a vision of hope.
Look well therefore to this day!
Such is the salutation of the dawn.

Kalidasa

Our Child

Our child
Now this is the day.
Our child,
Into the daylight
You will go out standing.
Preparing for your day.
Our child, it is your day,
This day.
May your road be fulfilled.
May we live in your thoughts,
May we be the ones whom your thoughts will embrace,
May you help us all to finish our roads.

Zuni Indian blessing

A Blessing of Iona

Deep peace of the running wave to you
Deep peace of the flowing air to you
Deep peace of the quiet earth to you
Deep peace of the shining stars to you
Deep peace of the Son of Peace to you

Children

Come to me, O ye children!
For I hear you at your play,
And the questions that perplexed me
Have vanished quite away.

Ye open the eastern windows,
That look towards the sun,
Where thoughts are singing swallows
And the brooks of morning run.

In your hearts are the birds and the sunshine,
In your thoughts the brooklet's flow,
But in mine is the wind of Autumn
And the first fall of the snow.

Ah! what would the world be to us
If the children were no more?
We should dread the desert behind us
Worse than the dark before.

What the leaves are to the forest,
With light and air for food,
Ere their sweet and tender juices
Have been hardened into wood,—

That to the world are children;
Through them it feels the glow
Of a brighter and sunnier climate
Than reaches the trunks below.

Come to me, O ye children!
And whisper in my ear
What the birds and the winds are singing
In your sunny atmosphere.

For what are all our contrivings,
And the wisdom of our books,
When compared with your caresses,
And the gladness of your looks?

Ye are better than all the ballads
That ever were sung or said;
For ye are living poems,
And all the rest are dead.

Henry Wadsworth Longfellow

The Upanishads

Lead us from death to life,
From falsehood to truth;
Lead us from despair to hope,
From fear to trust;
Lead us from hate to love,
From war to peace;
Let peace fill our hearts,
Our world, our universe.

If

If you can keep your head when all about you
Are losing theirs and blaming it on you,
If you can trust yourself when all men doubt you,
But make allowance for their doubting too;

If you can wait and not be tired by waiting,
Or being lied about, don't deal in lies,
Or being hated, don't give way to hating,
And yet don't look too good, nor talk too wise:

If you can dream—and not make dreams your master;
If you can think—and not make thoughts your aim;
If you can meet with Triumph and Disaster
And treat those two impostors just the same;

If you can bear to hear the truth you've spoken
Twisted by knaves to make a trap for fools,
Or watch the things you gave your life to, broken,
And stoop and build 'em up with worn-out tools:

If you can make one heap of all your winnings
And risk it on one turn of pitch-and-toss,
And lose, and start again at your beginnings
And never breathe a word about your loss;

If you can force your heart and nerve and sinew
To serve your turn long after they are gone,
And so hold on when there is nothing in you
Except the Will which says to them: 'Hold on!'

If you can talk with crowds and keep your virtue,
Or walk with Kings—nor lose the common touch,
If neither foes nor loving friends can hurt you,
If all men count with you, but none too much;

If you can fill the unforgiving minute
With sixty seconds' worth of distance run,
Yours is the Earth and everything that's in it,
And—which is more—you'll be a Man, my son!

Rudyard Kipling

Boundless be your Love

Do not deceive, do not despise each other anywhere. Do not be angry nor bear secret resentments; for as a mother will risk her life and watches over her child, so boundless be your love to all, so tender, kind and mild.

Cherish good will right and left, early and late, and without hindrance, without stint, be free of hate and envy, while standing and walking and sitting down, whatever you have in mind, the rule of life that is always best is to be loving-kind.

Buddha

From **This Child, My Child**

This child, my child, with a smile that beams,
I wish for him contentment, fulfilment of dreams.
I give him my love with all that I do,
And guide him through life, with goals to pursue.

Our memories should hold, such a colourful display,
Of first words, first steps, and first times at play.
Make each day important, don't push him too fast,
Take time and enjoy him, make each moment last.
Your child needs love, as much as you do,
Give love to your child, and he'll return it to you.

Anon

Other books from Montpelier Publishing available through Amazon

Body, Mind and Spirit

Non-Religious Wedding Readings
The Simple Living Companion
Non-Religious Funeral Readings
Marriage Advice
How to be Happy

Frugal living

Frontier Frugal
A Treasury of Thrift
The Men's Guide to Frugal Grooming
1001 Ways to Save Money
Gardening Tips
The Frugal Gentleman

Humour and puzzles

Wedding Jokes
The Book of Church Jokes
After Dinner Laughs
After Dinner Laughs 2
Scottish Jokes
A Little Book of Limericks
The Bumper Book of Riddles, Puzzles and Rhymes
Welsh Jokes

Men's Interest

The Pipe Smoker's Companion
Advice to Gentlemen
The Real Ale Companion
The Cigar Collection

Travel

The Dalai Lama Next Door
The Slow Bicycle Companion
Poems of London

19081070R00033

Printed in Great Britain
by Amazon